HEADWATERS

HEADWATERS
Poems & Field Notes

Saul Weisberg

Pleasure Boat Studio
New York

First printing

Pleasure Boat Studio: A Literary Press
201 West 89th Street
New York, NY 10024
Tel/Fax 413-677-0085
www.pleasureboatstudio.com

ISBN: 9780912887159
Library of Congress Control Number: 2014912265
Weisberg, Saul 1953 –
[Poems. Selections]
Headwaters: Poems & Field Notes by Saul Weisberg

Cover (*Pyramid Peak, Diablo Lake*) and illustrations adapted from original art by Molly Hashimoto, www.mollyhashimoto.com

Author photo by Benj Drummond, www.bdsjs.com

Book design by Jessica Haag

For Shelley

CONTENTS

NATURAL HISTORY

WALKING INTO MOUNTAINS

ENCOUNTERS

HOME GROUND

FIELD NOTES

NATURAL HISTORY

All Trees Are Alone

All trees are alone
and will bear children alone
in the dark.

The ecstasy of conifers,
a swell of tenderness
in the valley.

Long silent passion –
the seduction of naked seeds,
soft brush of pollen.

The infinite ache
of wood becoming
wood.

ELECTION DAY

Sagebrush trembles,
crisp morning breeze,
sunrise over the pines.

Paddling the lake at first light,
small flocks of coots along the shore,
everyone is talking.

The morning after the election
eight white swans
graze dark fields by the river.

CHICKADEE

Chickadee –
such a tiny bundle of hope.

A few words
on a torn scrap of paper
blown into cottonwoods
along the river.

If not for hunger, or love,
what is anything for?

SANDPIPER SUITE

Curlew, plover, sanderling, snipe,
dunlin, turnstone, dowitcher, knot,
whimbrel, godwit, yellowlegs, ruff,
willet, tattler, phalarope, stilt.
Even their names are beautiful.

All our songs
crying out in the night.
The smaller birds are silent.

Along twisted coastlines,
forgotten bays and islands,
cobbled beaches, sandflats, mud,
full moon and cloud haze.

Restlessness shared of summer wings,
long legs quick in half-light,
probing bill curved to follow what moves,
yielding to flight,
quick flash to morning sky.

Wheeling flock trains itself south,
tides beckon and fall away.
Horizons call with land's end
ten thousand miles and three weeks away.

CROWS

Afternoon count –
two, then four, now six
crows on a bare branch.

Talking about the war –
eight crows eat breakfast
on the riverbank.

Ten crows flying –
the pattern of their passing
forms and breaks against the sky.

Someone once told me
that any number of things
can be described by a ratio:

I'm not sure that applies to crows.

Owl, Wren and Crow

Full moon –
the barn owl's face,
bright in the night.

Deep within the forest,
song of Pacific wren –
quick splashes of light.

One hundred crows –
tattered brush strokes
across the sky.

Autumn Camp, Ross Lake

Every morning, a few more
crinkled red leaves
of the vine maples
appear on the trail
to the water.

JUNIPER

In the desert
I seek shade,
and in its cool embrace,
notice for the first time
the perfect berries
of the juniper.

ALL TAXA BIOLOGICAL INVENTORY

And when we have learned
the names of all the ten thousand beings,
what then?

Now, can we begin to talk about love?

DATURA

Surrounded by datura
and the desert river –
our tent.

Inside, all night,
what dreams
we share!

ON THE HOH RIVER

On the braided gravel bar
eight elk sit on folded knees.

Children of the mist
rise and walk into darkness.

The river gathers friends
on its way to the sea.

WE WAKE TO THE SOUND OF BEES

We lie in our sleeping bags
in a valley of rock and sage
as dawn unfolds the colors of the night.

We wake to the sound of bees
that have found the water
you set out for our morning coffee.

Tightly packed into a battered aluminum pot,
a full quart of yellow and black bodies
begins to boil.

Trapped between bees and rock,
we pull our jackets up to our chins,
confused and amazed.

Within minutes the water is gone
and small drops of living liquid
fly into the light.

CANYON SPRING

Following the shade line
downstream through cool water
my bare feet still hurt
from yesterday's 14-mile hike.

Red cliffs, oak groves,
sudden splashes of green.
Beneath maidenhair fern
small fish dart for cover.

KINGFISHER

Around each bend of the river
kingfisher waits
for my canoe.

Quick pump of wings,
fast rise and fall of flight,
loud rattle from the farthest tree.

Am I following kingfisher or chasing him?

It's all a game to kingfisher
who leads me to the cove
where the first skunk cabbage blooms.

ECHO

In 1934 the last O'o sang
from the slopes of Mauna Loa
and listened for the song of its mate.

The song, half of a lonely duet,
rang through the forest.
The bird waited for an answer.

I wonder how long he kept singing?

Twenty years earlier
the last passenger pigeon died
in a Cincinnati zoo.

Billions became thousands,
hundreds became one,
and the slaughter was complete.

The skies were silent.

And now, one hundred years later,
the skies grow warmer,
hundreds of species flicker into the dark.

The echo of birds,
golden frogs, coral reefs,
all the creatures whose names we will never know.

I wonder: What does it mean to become extinct?

The Stone Knife

Long ago, they used them every day.
Blade still sharp against my thumb,
I leave it beside the rock.

Archaeology tells us
the old ones
were once young.

Sitting in a stone shelter,
waiting for mountain goats,
talking about love.

Bee in the Net

Without warning
        the bee releases
                the heat of the sun –
from star to sky,
        leaf to nectar,
                to living insect,
deep
        into the palm
                of my hand.
I burn
        with the heat
                of a distant star.

Naturalist

On the mountain, through sun-drenched talus,
you chased a bird all day
until you found its name
    – rock wren.

In the marsh, the mosquitoes were fierce,
and still you stood at the water's edge
looking for those last field marks
    – black tern.

We learn together:
intimate relations
are worth a little pain.

Warming Trend

Thin crescents of snow
just below the summit:
all that's left in a dry year.
Sheets of polished bedrock
feel sun for the first time.
Northwest mountains
emerge into light.

The Weight of Sunlight

Hangs heavy between the pines,
cold boulders creep toward the light.

Dragonfly hesitates, then turns
down the bright ribbon of the creek.

I follow your shadow through shallow water,
cobbled rocks smooth against my feet.

A merganser flies upstream,
white patches of reflected sunlight.

We move slowly to higher ground,
seeking a path around the mountain.

White Birds of Winter

On the delta of the Skagit River
there are flocks of snow geese 10,000 strong:

> wing-strong,
> > wind-strong,

rising, then settling
on silent fields.

The sun melts into the ocean,
waves cast shadows on the beach,
everything stands still.

Six swans,
the ones that flew over our tent last night,
settle in the lagoon behind the dunes.

Bugs

I chase butterflies
through clouds
of mosquitoes.

Yellow leaves on black water,
blue dragonfly rattles wings
low over the marsh.

Monarchs –
tall grass prairie,
orange wings above the lake.

I think it's a dragonfly –
the last falling leaf
of the alder.

Trying to read poems
over the din of the waterfall:
six white butterflies circle the pines.

The dragonfly pauses –
a piece of the swallowtail's wing
drifts to the ground.

From a hole in the belly of the dead snake
the orange and black carrion beetle
looks out at the world.

Another summer,
another summit,
waving my net at bugs.

BARELY AUGUST

Already the yellow leaves
of the alders
have begun to fall.

Everywhere I go –
spotted sandpipers
along the riverbank.

MIGRATION

Fresh snow,
the high calls of warblers
enter the valley.

The journey continues,
small wings beat steadily
through still air.

Small Bones

I dream in the peaks
of small birds singing
deep in the forest.

Far below, in the river,
the bones of small birds
are drifting toward the sea.

Its Song Moves Upstream

Between two waterfalls on the frozen creek
the small nest of a dipper –
wreathed in moss and fern.

Under thin ice
the absence of color
moves swiftly.

Four Songs

Thrush –
sings a waterfall over mossy cliff
into a still pool.

Woodpecker –
taps in triplets
deep in the woods.

Water ouzel –
tumbles downstream,
eddies between the rocks.

Canyon wren –
bounces through the desert
from cliff to crag.

SEARCH IMAGE
for Thea Linnaea Pyle

The eggs of lycaenid butterflies
are so small
and you found so many
under the leaves of flowers
across the shadowed hillside.

Echo Blue
    Brown Elfin
        Spring Azure.

You were always looking
for small beauties.

BUTTERFLIES TASTE WITH THEIR FEET

In summer, the fritillary
lays its eggs
where next year's violets will bloom.

On the dry floor of the forest
small bits of protoplasm
dance in the sun.

The Medium of Song is Air

All night we hear thin calls and chips
pass over us in the dark.
The cats listen from the window ledge.

In the morning we wake to find
great clouds of migrating passerines
settled in the maples by the creek.

Their songs fill the house and fields
as if air itself could sing.

Spring Music

All you need to know
    about my day:

winter wren
    in the morning,

canyon wren
    at dusk.

WALKING INTO MOUNTAINS

HEADWATERS

With cupped hands
I bow and drink

each day
a different stream

many times
from the same river

and once,
the sea.

CLIMBING TALUS

Third week of August,
already the first snow
has come and gone.

How good to stretch my legs
on warming east slope
morning talus trail.

The path steepens –
a hermit thrush
sings from the spire of subalpine fir.

Together, these rocks seem stable,
but each can move,
and does, often.

Balance each foot in turn,
stones suspended
on their way to the sea.

Obsessed with balance
we grow, we fall;
call it virtue.

My feet carry me so far,
and the river's cold embrace
the only gratitude I can offer.

SEPTEMBER STORM, ROSS LAKE
for John Miles

The green canoe
waits in the rain.
Walking in clouds,
no one hears our footsteps.

Hanging on the end of the fir bough,
raindrop eye of the nuthatch.
Between two maple branches,
the spider's web catches rain.

Too lazy to walk to the lake,
we place a kettle under the dripping tarp.
Waiting for tea to steep,
I turn the page.

The forest grows dark,
light rests on the lake.
Whitecaps move slowly,
clouds of memories along the shore.

Mountains Turn to Winter

Even in October,
the sound of snowmelt
water flowing over stone.

This morning is too cold
for bumblebees.

Huckleberries thick with summer sugar,
raven's wings like torn silk,
mares' tails drift from the south.

The sky is empty until it fills itself
with birds and light.
The long day passes slowly.

On the shadowed trail
the evening sun lights your face.
Tomorrow's snow begins to fall.

The wind leans against me.
I carry its song close to my chest.

East of the Mountains

Wild rhododendron
in the Oregon hills,
fog rolling in.

Suddenly –
the desert.

Cottonwoods
along the river.

Desert Morning

We rise and wait
for the sun's warmth,
our hands clasped around
steaming mugs of tea.

We spend the next fourteen hours
seeking shade.

SAHALE MORAINE

White remnant of glacial ice,
curve of gray rock
unwinds to meet the sky.

A thin line
of mountain hemlock
follows the moraine into clouds.

Above timberline
we pause between two branches
of a foaming creek.

Across the valley
marmots whistle,
then silence.

Small creeks gather
at the headwaters
of the cirque.

Far below, a green ridge of heather,
and a snowmelt stream,
almost too faint to hear.

Luminescent clouds
rise from the valley,
drift toward distant waterfalls.

It feels good
to walk uphill on sun-warmed rocks.
All trails lead to mountains.

BOSTON BASIN BIVOUAC

Half-filled moon over Cascade Peak,
pale sun sinks behind Dorado Needle,
slopes of Sahale and Sharkfin grow red.

Small stove, rice noodles simmer,
a cup of strong black tea.
My penny whistle mixes with the wind.

Marsh hawk low over the moraine,
sleeping bag spread on white rock slab,
I wait for Orion to rise.

In the center
of a ring of peaks
in the center of the world.

SMALL DELIGHTS, FISHER BASIN

Hike eighteen miles
with a heavy pack
in a light rain
to sit on a log
in the middle of a creek
eating a tangerine.

Forbidden Peak, Northwest Face

A thin granite rib rises from the glacier
and splits the mountain in two.

We follow a simple line of rock and ice
into a cloudless sky.

Frozen in silence
crystals hold the edges together.

From the summit
we see the approaching storm.

Albert Camp

Ruby-crowned kinglets
sing from tree to tree.

Wind blows ice crystals
across the meadows.

I look out over miles
of green forest turning white.

Silence,
    wind,
        birdsong.

DESOLATION LOOKOUT

I wake in the night,
an owl calls from the forest.
At first light, a distant loon.

Fresh snow on Nohokomeen,
icy morning hands,
moon sets over the Pickets.

We leave cedars behind at the lake,
race clouds and sunlight
up the mountain.

Two redtails
circle upwards screaming,
west slope lake wind.

Friends out of sight,
above me on the trail,
so much beauty, each step new.

The last few steps to the lookout,
you can't go any higher.
Empty bowl of sky, peaks hang from clouds.

The lake fills the valley.
Spires of subalpine fir rise through the mist.
We are surrounded by stories.

HARTS PASS

We climb through black shale cliffs
and rock gardens
until lowering clouds turn cold and fall.

We descend into the fragrance
of hail-bruised flowers
that rise in clouds of color.

BOOKS FOR THE PACK

Before our journey into mountains
we choose by size and weight
the books that we place in our packs.

I pick four, and wedge them tight
between climbing gear and cook pots:
    Basho's *Haiku*, Mathews' *Natural History*,
    Sund's *Ish River*, Pyle's *Butterflies*.

What rests on the pages is weightless.

Canyon Storm, Escalante River

The shadow of a swift –
flash of black blade
across red sandstone.

From sun to shade,
sudden clouds and thunder,
the first drops of rain.

Suddenly,
from high canyon walls,
dozens of waterfalls.

Our legs move
like lightning –
downstream.

TRAILS THAT TURN TO STONE

Three kestrels scream
high above the summit;
the wind must be fierce up there.

They soar into the west, and
I resume my slow descent
into the world.

This dance of boot on rock,
each step placed just right,
then left behind, forgotten.

So many years of climbing
trails that turn to stone
and disappear.

LITTLE BEAVER CREEK

All day we watched the storm arrive,
our candle burns clear in the still evening.

Raven calls – a low pitched gurgle above our tent,
I fall asleep listening for wind.

Heating water for morning tea,
the lake like shattered glass.

ONCE AGAIN

The old trail follows the creek
past ancient trees
and the sound of water.

The sky clears, light fades,
varied thrushes sing their two-note song
deep within the forest.

Once again,
like visiting friends,
I walk into familiar mountains.

PATH BETWEEN ISLANDS
for Kurt Hoelting

The waterfall tumbles over the rock ledge.
The mind chatters,
that's just what it does.

How long has it been
since I was quiet and alone
in the woods?

A busy mind cannot heal itself,
right now –
sound of falling water.

My shadow,
the tree's shadow,
soon both will be gone.

Paying attention,
not paying attention,
it's all the same.

A little cricket
has entered this poem.

First Snow

Wind stirs
white flowers
above the rocky trail.

High in the mountains
the first snow falls.
Rivers tremble in their sleep.

I follow you
to a pool of snowmelt water.
Shadowed basin, stone cold.

Grazing the Huckleberries

Moss covers the ground like green fur.
Trails follow cedars back from the lake.
We seek the red huckleberries
that cling to the smallest branches.

Our lips separate each berry,
leaves and stems fall away,
grazing and laughing –
this is serious business.

Late at night, in a tiny bed,
wondering at this unexpected
warmth, I dream of red fruit.

Ascending Heather Pass

Clouds in the valley,
blue on the summit,
sun and shadows.

Last night's rain –
at the center of each leaf,
a single pool of light.

Three miles and still climbing,
I come upon an old woman
hiking with backpack and crutches.

Unsure of how to pass on the narrow trail
I walk slowly, fifty feet behind.
When she stops, bends over, I kick stones.

She looks up, smiles, and exclaims
"The violets are so blue!"
Her eyes, sparkling, are also blue.

CONFLUENCE CAMP, PARIA RIVER

Too tired for love,
we lie next to each other
in our camp below the confluence –
a great tumble of rocks above our heads.

From our sleeping bags
we watch the stars of the Great Bear
pour from a high crack
and wade the length of the river.

The moon brings shadows,
the river grows dark,
a few birds call,
our hands touch drowsily in the night.

In early morning a soft light
brings red cliffs to life.
White-throated swifts throw
themselves into the sky.

Mountain Hemlock

"Look at the stars," you said,
"the whole tree is covered with stars."

And it was true –
tiny whorls of needles
glistening in reflected light.

Ever since that time,
I don't remember where or when,
I always look for the stars,
and seeing them, see your laughing face.

So today, high in a cirque basin
at timberline, with granite and
waterfalls all around,

I see one small orange and black butterfly
a fritillary, fanning its wings
on a stunted mountain hemlock.

The whole night sky reflected there,
and where are you?

WALKING INTO MOUNTAINS

Walking into mountains
in the rain,
deeper and deeper,
everything is green.

Climbing into a clear light,
absence of sound and birds,
on the crest of the ridge,
one rock melted free of snow.

ENCOUNTERS

Cabeza Prieta

This light,
like no other morning,
just before the sun
rises over the desert.

As we have done so many times before,
in mountains, ocean, desert,
we sit hunched on the ground
writing in journals.

The years go by,
and our words still walk with us
into the wind.

THREE CORNER ROCK LOOKOUT

My flute echoes across green hills,
coyotes fall silent.
Wind drifts music down the river
after swallows.

Darkness grows
like a hand in the west.
The trees sigh as if
released from struggle.

How wonderful to wake
among clouds smelling of the sea.
A solid layer of stratus below me,
above, cumulus rise into blue sky.

After five days of ninety degree heat
I dream of shearwaters banking low over the waves.
I smell the open light
of birds clinging to an azure sky.

The hills lost in haze,
volcanic up-thrusts shout with snow and rock.
When the sun goes down
the wind begins slowly from the east.

Night birds sing from the huckleberries
around my lookout.

TRAIL WORK

Long thin song
of winter wren
spills through
the forest.

The waterfalls
of distant peaks
move closer.

All day working on trails,
shoveling snow
above timberline.

In the evening,
over Mount Buckner,
the rose of a distant star
dims and dies.

They Could Be Flowers

We wake at sunrise
and walk into the cold light
of the desert morning.

In the shadow of the border fence
the desert blooms with colors.
Scattered over rocky ground,
lost, never in pairs – children's sneakers.

What does it mean to be very young,
to walk at night in a foreign land,
and lose your shoes?

It's Not Just the Economy

When the world shrieks with hatred and greed
I go paddling on a nearby lake
and listen to wrens sing from the forest,
hear the heavy splash of a loon taking flight
and a father comforting a child fallen on the rocky path.

We have so little time
and so much work to do,
why waste it on hate and war?

LOST MOUNTAIN
for Tim McNulty

From the porch
where I sleep
the valley drops toward the river
then rises into range after range
of green hills.

At first light
birdsong spirals
toward the higher peaks.

DAYS LIKE THIS

Days like this
I wish I was a bird –
quick flash of wing,
flat silence of mud and sky.

We sit on the edge
of quickly beating joy,
pointed toward
distant horizons.

Northwest Winds

Fresh gale in the bay,
spindrift blows in streaks
across the waves.

I can't get the boat off the beach,
sit at home by the window
looking out at the rain.

Crouched on barnacled rocks,
hunchbacked turnstones
take refuge in the lee of the wind.

Small black and white bodies
wait it out,
no other place to go.

SALISH SEA

Surf-laughter,
rocky headlands,
outer coast
curls back on itself.

Curves –
a dory marks the stillness of the bay.
Too far away to see,
indistinct man-form, moving oars.

Flute song,
breathing music,
sound of a shorebird's wing.
Air, like water – thick, dripping.

Islands alone:
rocks, reefs, foam,
afternoon rain,
red cedar along the shore.

Clearing on the horizon,
wind from the southwest,
loons diving –
stillness.

PADDLES

The yellow canoe
tied on top of the red car
next to the frozen lake.

Drifting –
it's all right in a canoe,
in life, another story.

Sometimes
when my mind wanders
only the canoe goes straight.

I point my paddle
where I want to go,
the wind has other ideas.

At the edge of the ice
the canoe hovers,
tasting winter.

Sounds Rising Like Gulls

My body is made
of dark colors
and the sounds
of whales rolling
in the depths of the sea.

When the sun rises
I descend through
layers of water
falling like snow
and hide in deep ocean trenches
for weeks without sleep.

At dusk seabirds gather
to wait for the tide.
When I dream
I hear sounds
rising like gulls.

BONE

When we become bone,
and by that I mean scapula,
laid out, flat and white
on some remembered beach
drifting on silent tides.

I don't mean that
kind of bone, but real –
I said scapula,
flat and that terribly dried
hard kind of white that
means a long time dead.

What I mean is that
when we become bone
it's over.

STONE TOOLS

Flint, agate, obsidian, chert –
for love we have all been broken.

Discarded along the trail,
small piles of chipped stone.

Some of us may yet be pounded
and flaked into useful lives.

WALKING MEDITATION

Three horses in winter rain
backs slicked wet and steaming.

I walk quietly through an overgrown field
paying attention to my breathing.

I look down, and see my shoes
covered in horseshit.

FISHERMAN'S SONG TO THE SHEARWATER

From Destruction Island to the Columbia Bar,
Astoria to Coos Bay, we follow the salmon.
Green swells lift from astern,
the boat shudders as the waves pass.

To the east, the Olympics glisten through fog,
the western horizon always receding.
From the northwest, with the wind
shearwaters glide between sea and sky.

Brown scimitar, flash of pale wing linings,
thin black bill and hooked tube-nose.
Knowing endless distance:
sun, stars, moon and storms.

Stranger to land –
shearwater.

Mount Shuksan

Above Price Lake
we work together
under towering ice cliffs
recovering the bodies
of two young men
killed by an avalanche
while climbing
the north face.

Across the valley
twin waterfalls
cascade in silence
over gray rock.

What we carry away is flesh,
what remains is color and light.

Storm at La Push

The storm blew all night.
Rain fell like thrown gravel
on the cabin's metal roof.

Windows rattle,
we seek each other's warmth
beneath dark wool.

In the morning I light the woodstove,
pour a cup of tea, watch you sleep,
your hair like tossed wheat.

Crows wade through rain-splashed puddles,
a white-haired Indian man in a denim jacket
walks past carrying a cloth bag full of tools.

Moonlight

Shallow sliver
    of crescent moon
reflects twice –

once
    on cloud,
once, again,
    on white-capped sea.

WILD DUCK

We did not hear the guns
when the wild duck fell
in the frozen marsh.

The dogs found her
twenty feet from the trail
as we walked away from the sun.

In our kindness
it took a long time
for us to kill her.

Removing feathers, head and feet,
we made her somewhat less,
until what remained we cooked and ate.

It was later,
in the dark,
that I dreamed of flight.

Rivers

All across Ohio,
    rivers connecting
clouds,
    small farms and tractors,
everywhere
    loops of water, ringed islands,
snaked
    brown rivers, checkered fields,
dendritic branches.
    The land muscles
as it reaches water.
    Slow rivers,
green rivers,
    I am in love with water.

Centuries

Mountains wait,
they gather rain,
salmon and cedar
move north.
After a long time
the light changes
and something
new comes along.
No one knows
what happens next.

How We Spend Our Time
for Tom Fleischner

All night,
deep in the backcountry –
desert moon and shadows.

In the morning we drink tea,
walk for water,
look for birds in an empty sky.

In the afternoon
we sit in the shade of ironwood
and talk of wives, lovers and friends.

Together,
we grow older
on the same stories.

CASCADE PASS

In the distance, at the pass,
I see you and raise my hand
high over my head,
palm open in greeting.

What memories
move through our minds
at that moment?
We smile and bow together.

HOME GROUND

Even More Beautiful

The wind has blown the red leaves
of the maples into the corner of the yard.
They are even more beautiful in the rain.

We had been fighting
and you asked me to sit with you
on the warm rocks overlooking the bay.

WOODSTOVE

After three days
without heat
my wife and I
light the new woodstove
for the first time
and lie together
watching the cat
stretch and sprawl
across the red tiles
of the hearth.

AUTUMN LEAVES

Two red leaves from the plum tree
blew in with last night's rain
through the open window above our bed.

In the morning, they rest,
paired with raindrops
on your breasts.

AGE

No mirrors remain at the old homestead,
only rain-filled barrels
surrounded by maples.

What happens when we get old?
We wake in the morning
and pull on wrinkled gloves.

Late morning shower –
you wash away the past,
wet footprints on the porch.

The last gold leaves
cling to the white branches
of the aspen.

PELTON BASIN
for Shelley

Moonlight touches the ridge-crest,
fresh snow dusts the peaks,
cold September stars paint
the shadows of the night.

In the midst of all this bright beauty,
your smiling face, dancing eyes,
curves of breast and belly –
    tasting the darkness,
    tasting the mountains.

Gentle woman, to wake again
nestled in your arms
would be all I ask,
to kiss the hollow of your neck,
a blessing.

SOLSTICE

In a meadow
at the edge of timberline
I wake to the spring song
of the chickadee
and remember you
teaching me the names of flowers
before we married.

WHITE SHELL

A white shell on a white sand beach,
sound of waves in the moonlight.

Your blue eyes looking up at me,
our rhythmic rocking.

A sandpiper's cry
brightens the darkness.

End of Summer

The cries of migrating swans
stitch the clouds together,
white on white.

Rain yesterday,
sun this afternoon,
cold trees shedding leaves.

In the brown reeds
a red-winged blackbird
remembers his summer song.

Each stroke of my paddle
brings me closer
to those I love.

COLLECTIONS

Throughout our home,
we have placed them with random care
in bowls and baskets:

small stones from distant beaches,
a cairn of green sea-glass two inches tall,
pieces of driftwood, angled bits of bone,
juniper berries, owl feathers,
an otter's skull, and the dried eggs and nest
of a white-crowned sparrow.

We make our memories
from their stories.

What Fathers Do

In the cold night,
after the lights are dark,
I check again the quiet rooms,
the gas stove, the cats,
and the locks on all the doors
before climbing the stairs
past the sleeping rooms
of my children.

Imagining Rain

Once, unable to sleep,
my daughter imagined rain –
all night, gusts in the trees,
ripples on the windows,
a gentle drumming on the roof.

HOLE-IN-THE-WALL, RIALTO BEACH

That's where the full moon comes from,
says my daughter.

A window into
another world.

We can pass
straight on through to the other side.

YOU MIGHT NOT REMEMBER

You were nine when you saw
your first shooting star –

a clear summer night
moon almost full,

snow on peaks,
sister sleeping by your side.

ALVORD DESERT

Sun sinks behind desert mountains,
horizons in all directions.

Orange moon rising,
full, perfect.

Our children spinning,
dancing cartwheels.

Your hair covers your bare shoulders
like a cloth flecked with salt and sand.

All night long,
a warm wind from the west.

PARIA CANYON

Soft repetitive calls,
insects in the night.
The sky sinks from blue to black,
stars begin to appear.

We lay our books aside, turn off our headlamps,
you place your leg over mine.
We could fall off the earth
into the stars.

CATS

In the night room
the green eyes of the cat
deep in the belly of the chair.

Hit by a car when she was young –
the awkward gallop
of the three-legged cat.

In the valley that lies
between our thighs
the young cat stretches, preens and purrs.

The blind cat
flattens to the ground
when the barred owl calls.

DISTANCES

The space between two bodies touching,
how large it seems –
nearly wide enough for a river to pour through,
or raise a range of new mountains,
peaks grasping at the sky.

REMEMBERING STORIES WE WERE TOLD
for Irv Weisberg

When you died
we lost all your stories.
Why did I believe
they would last forever?

Your hands are still,
holding all those memories
that we let slip
through our fingers.

An hour before sunrise,
we wait for that quiet space
to fill with bird song
and the sound of falling water.

The candle flickers
each time someone
enters the room.

GOLDFINCHES

One of my father's gifts
was the joy that would light his face
when he saw something beautiful:

Goldfinches in the spring,
morning waves on a lake,
a sunset glimpsed through trees.

He smiled with his lips pulled back
as if the bright flash of beauty
had seared him with its sudden heat.

Then he would turn his head
to make sure
that we had seen it too.

Three Dreams

1.

All night I dreamed of him,
looking into my eyes on that last evening,
stricken with pain and wonder –
that terrible moment.
    What comes next?
    He knows.

2.

My wife dreams
my father did not die,
but merely stopped talking,
and then, in her dream, he began to speak.
    "What was he saying?"
    "That wasn't in the dream."

3.

My mother dreams
my father was having a nightmare
and she was trying to wake him.
Then she remembers he's dead
and it must be her nightmare.

INCISIONS

Biopsy –
this is how we measure
the meaning of love.

Twice this past year
the surgeon's scalpel has touched
the breasts of those I love.

LAYAH

A marmot whistles –
another, higher in the basin, answers.
On the other side of the world
my mother visits her dying sister.
Two ravens cross the ridge crest
and disappear.

FRIENDS

We watch the silhouettes of pines
as the last dim light
fades behind the mountains.

It is this long sharing of stories and wine,
desert walks and the pull of shared labor
that nourish our friendship.

DITCH CREEK

Early morning sun pours through the pines.
We stop together at a cabin beneath mountains
to help an old friend put in his winter's wood.

Snow squeaks under our boots.
We follow tracks of coyote, weasel and hare
through the forest.

Rounds of split pine spin through the air
and land with a hollow thud
in the bed of the pickup.

We walk together to the cabin,
pass the wood from hand to hand,
build the crib head-high, four rows deep.

Late in the evening, by the fire,
we drink wine, and talk of things
illuminated and warmed by stories.

No Straight Lines

There are no straight lines
in the lives of birds
or dancers' bodies.

The sun on still water
traces paths
of reflected light
across the wrinkles
that surround my eyes.

There is no way
I can construct
a pain that would
be as solid and straight
as an iron rod.

Or a love
that could be carved
like white pine.

TAXI-MAN

Running for a taxi at the Austin airport,
the taxi-man, with gray ponytail and missing incisor,
motions me into the front seat of an old Crown Victoria,
the back scattered with paper and books.
He watches as I turn to look at a flock of birds
under the shrubs at the edge of the freeway.

A few minutes later he pulls off the road,
passes a pair of battered binoculars to me,
and points toward a cell tower
where a great colony of monk parakeets
have covered the metal structure with loose stick nests.

We sit for a long moment watching birds
as angry traffic zooms past.
He tells me of a "sea of blue-green wings" moving north
these past five years, then turns on the radio
and violins fill the cab.

The rest of the way into Austin, we talk about those
beautiful wings and music from the other side of the world.
We don't always know what we think we know,
until someone shows us, and we listen.

BRIDE OF NATURE

We walk over sun-washed hills,
our arms full of dried flowers
heavy with seed.

As the sun goes behind the mountains
you turn to me, exclaiming:
"I am a bride of nature."

This is what all that sunlight has become,
plants crumble into dust
blown before the wind.

I am the groom
wearing a single, yellow-bright dandelion,
standing by the side of the trail.

LEFT AT PATEROS
for Brian Scheuch

The long road into the mountains begins here,
you can't turn back now.

Fifty years later, you remember the delights of home,
and think of all the other paths you might have taken.

The road climbs toward sunlight
and the headwaters of your life.

We all know what's at the end of that road:
no need to rush.

AFTER 9.11

After a long week
filled with fear, and what comes after,
I paddle with my daughter
into the heart of the lake.

We pull the canoe
into sheltering reeds
and sit quietly
watching dark colors appear
in still water.

Night

I follow your shadow
through shallow water.
With each breath
the night comes closer.

Evening light fades,
our words grow dark.
Songs of thrushes
rise from the trees.

Beneath the shoulders of the forest,
the blooms of small orchids
delight me more
because of you.

Cotton sheathes your breasts
moon-light candles
quick cry heart-beat
shadows waiting
slow
moon-rise
rain.

SURPRISE

You light a candle
in the dark tent
and our shadows
dance on the rainfly.

When you
take me
in the night
only my mind
is surprised.

LISTENING TO SILENCE
for Rotha Miles

On the last day of November
light leaves the earth too soon.

The forest walks into winter,
winged seeds cling to the maples.

Goldeneye leave rippled trails
as they rise from the lake,
wing-whistle overhead.

At least a dozen species of lichen and moss
crowd the twisted branch of the fallen alder,
one hundred shades of gray and green.

Bird calls –
kinglets, bushtits, chickadees,
an eagle on the far shore.

Magic light tonight:
clouds glow under suffused sun,
lake-mist rises like tendrils of lost hair.

The lake is absolutely still –
listening to silence.

PRAIRIE FIRE
for Mary Jean Wiegert

It will snow soon. The afternoon forest
is alive with the gathering storm.
Juncos and chickadees cling to the snowberry,
a towhee rustles in the underbrush.
Your gray ashes settle into the cool earth.

In a circle of friends, Bruce's voice rises over the graves;
I have never heard him sing before.
We wait in silence for your answer.

It should not be this hard for us to let you go –
as it was for you to let go. We remember prairie fire and
bison, food trucks, your laugh, ocean minerals, the stars in
your bones. My handprint rests in the dirt of your grave.

What choices do we have before the storm?
Birds find shelter in the forest. Mist seeks us
among the trees. The fire burns
as you once burned with life.
We eat soup, drink wine, share stories.
A lake dimpled with rain is our offering.

Thirty Years

Because the road was closed
below the trailhead
you hiked ten miles in autumn rain
to meet me in the mountains
before you left for graduate school
in California.

This morning
our children camp in mountains
and walk ocean beaches
while we wake together
under September sky.

Home Ground

It's good to have a lake close to home,
also rivers, mountains too.
Familiar terrain and the comfort
of well-traveled trails.
In my pocket,
on the torn corner of a map –
directions to a place called home.

FIELD NOTES
Spring

The spring blush
of red huckleberries
makes the whole forest tremble.

Blown leaf tumbles uphill –
somewhere close, young birds in a nest,
loud, then still.

Monterey pines hang in heavy silence
absent the weight
of a million monarch wings.

The sky grows dark,
chattering calls of cliff swallows –
small flickers of light.

For two hours
before sunlight enters the valley –
the tanager's song.

Like a dark ribbon –
the song of Swainson's thrush
unrolls from the forest.

Twigs of last year's reeds
hold tatters
of last year's feathers.

In a valley of balsamroot
a meadowlark's song
flies from yellow to yellow.

On the western shore
the first unfolding leaves
light up the forest.

Deep in the marsh a towhee sings –
at the edge of memory
another answers.

Motionless –
the heron kills the fish
by waiting.

A living crescent crosses the moon –
the cry of migrating geese
dark against the sky.

Below the footbridge
a white egret
stands in my shadow.

Little cricket
how did you
enter my room?

Spring on the river –
an old man reads poems from his youth
surprised at each new word.

In the evening
alone in my tent –
the sound of the river.

Each time the otter dives
I crawl toward the tangled bank –
hear sharp teeth crunching bone.

Quiet morning in the garden,
nothing to do –
a deep breath tells us all we need to know.

Knife lesson –
small hands guide sharpened steel
for the first time.

Sitting in the garden
waiting for dogwood to bloom
my parents listen for warblers.

Helping my mother
down the steep slope to the lake
she holds tight to my hands.

Sisters –
two sets of footprints
walk up the beach.

Tonight, strawberries
the exact temperature
of the garden.

In the dark tent
I open my eyes just as you say –
do you want to feel something nice?

An empty net
like a blank page
holds promise.

I paddle slowly into the dark –
from the shoreline
cries of night birds follow me.

As the days grow longer
evening sun moves
to the wild side of the lake.

We don't need words
to know we are surrounded
by beauty.

Between rain showers
we sit around the fire
captured by light.

First night in the old hotel –
warm wind lifts the curtains
songs of new birds enter the room.

FIELD NOTES
Summer

Silences –
mountain summits, ocean depths
the spaces in between.

The fish the osprey dropped
flings itself onto the beach
again and again.

Samaras –
the weight of the forest
borne on the slender wings of maples.

On the whole hillside
three red huckleberries –
they were sweet.

Overnight, the talus slope comes alive –
red columbine nods
in the breeze.

In the center of each lupine leaf –
mist gathers a crystal drop
of dew.

Some have wings –
others are moved
by the wind.

Ravens over the summit –
their voices in the mountains
tell me I am home.

Thousands of small toads
all going somewhere
beneath the ferns.

Bright fish
break sunlight into a thousand silver coins
in the fisherman's net.

Lightning Creek –
thirty years ago
old friends drank this water.

Ripples –
the trace of her nipples lingers
on the still pond.

How good to drink
hot tea
in the shadow of pines.

Incessant calls:
many nuthatches
everywhere at once.

Evening shadows –
high in rocks
pika cries.

After long silence,
wind on pine,
unfolding leaf.

Small poems –
remnants of chipped stone
high in the mountains.

Canyon wren sings!
The desert holds its breath,
sun hides behind the mountain.

All the way up the trail
to the waterfall –
a lone hiker, whistling.

I sit beneath maples
listening to rain drip on leaves
bright with yesterday's sunlight.

So many nights lying in my tent
listening to the dark
opening of the world.

Deep in the mountains
at the bottom of my pack –
my lost house key.

I race home to show you the rainbow –
you're sitting on the porch
gazing at the sky.

We sit on the summit ridge –
the flame of a single match
burns clear between us.

Will my mother ever know
the daisies that grow in such abundance
in this mountain meadow?

Luna moth
rises into red oaks –
acorn caps make good whistles.

I love to watch
the strong muscles of your back
as our paddles pull us home.

One of the basic truths
of natural history –
sex is always better outside.

The paired calls of owls
wake us in the night –
what happens now?

After searching for a long time
I find my true religion –
song of the Swainson's thrush.

FIELD NOTES
Autumn

Leaves fall,
creeks enter the river,
the earth seeks sunlight.

What is it about the breath of pines?
Mist in the valley
new snow on the peaks.

In the river, a house of white bones –
skull and bleached vertebrae
of a fall Chinook.

The wild duck is black
inside the full circle
of the moon.

Not yet huckleberries –
green leaves hug the ground
larches drip, mist blows through.

From glacier to ocean
in three days. Upstream –
the sound of falling water.

I thought it was a flower –
red seed-head
of a saxifrage.

Autumn chill in the air –
only bumblebees
are out this morning.

Dew evaporates –
a spider's web catches
only sunlight.

"Listen," the river whispers
and what it says is
"here, now."

Colors fade –
night begins to climb
the other side of the hill.

Light falls
a blackbird calls from shore
the lake grows dark.

Old cedars
dream of the coast –
big canoes travel against the wind.

First snow in the mountains –
you say "beginner's mind"
but where to begin?

Sometimes, I am grateful
for the stories we hide
from each other.

A coastal stream
filled with raindrops –
small wooden bells.

My beard is gray –
I still like to walk
the storm-lit beach at night.

Pulling weeds
red beetles
lose their homes.

In nightgown and faded sweater
my wife carries the old cat
into the garden.

Cool mountain wind
my mind a swinging door
open and closed.

Foghorn –
all night, from the bay
the moon calls.

Everything is history –
only some of it
is remembered.

Conservation –
some days I don't give a shit about the planet:
it never lasts.

A moving shadow –
light pours
over the waterfall.

Green tea –
essence of leaves
and old sunlight.

What does it mean to forget?
I can't remember –
sunlit boulder by the river.

This trail knows
where it's going –
straight up!

After five days' rain –
a single dry feather
under my tent.

Raven's shadow changes shape:
fast black light
on red sandstone.

Time –
burning memories
as fast as it can.

FIELD NOTES
Winter

In the morning, fresh snow
and on the snow, fox tracks
white on white.

The dawn's light begins
with the strike of a match
held in your hand.

It was cold in the tent
when you lifted your shirt
to show me your breasts.

New moon,
trees wet with snow,
chickadee calls under the eaves.

Trees dressed in moss and shade:
a wren's song cries out
over and over in the night.

Seven days rain –
flood waters rise over the fields,
snow geese seen through clouds.

On the rocky shore
wing-feathers of a dead brant
lift in the wind.

Cold water –
a dipper's song
washes the rocks.

Walking around the volcano
rocks tell many stories –
only some of them are known.

Deep in the forest
the shelter roof
needs sweeping.

Snow, rain, mist and tears –
many forms
feed the living tissue.

Miles from camp
I rinse my mouth with seawater –
setting sun.

Everyday joy –
standing in winter wind
watching the moon.

The sculptor digs in his garden
to bury the broken stone corpse
of an arctic tern.

The Buddha's wife –
did anyone ask what she wanted?
The long nights pass slowly.

Heavy rain on the lake
louder than the wind
sound of torn cloth.

I walk the beach toward sunrise –
laughing gulls
have the last word.

So still,
I can barely see its breath –
the winter lake.

At every border
the homeless are reminded
of their home.

In the dark of winter
with the dawn –
a child's cry.

Empty boat
drifts in the white light
of the moon.

Late afternoon sun –
hemlock branches
bent under snow.

Clouds wander –
shadow of a river
glimpsed and gone.

At the creek's edge
a nuthatch's call
brings color, then fades.

Following my mother
on a trail through the woods
my brother carries my father's ashes.

A gift of rocks
balanced high
at the edge of the tide.

After work
on the dark lake
I paddle back to myself.

At sunset, three swans
fly from horizon to horizon –
white triangle in the sky.

The black bird
makes a hole in the sky
wherever it goes.

There are stories
waiting for someone –
it's your turn now.

Notes and Acknowledgments

I have always been drawn to mountains; I came late to the love of rivers. I was born near the East River on the lower east side of Manhattan, and spent my childhood close to Ohio's Cuyahoga River, which flamed on its way to Lake Erie. After college I followed friends and the writing of the beat poets to the Pacific Northwest. Our rivers rise from abundant rain, deep seasonal snowpack and the summer melt of glaciers. They flow through mountains, meadows and forests on their way to the Pacific.

I came to the Northwest in my twenties and worked, mostly outside, doing whatever it took to keep me in this special part of the world: commercial fishing, fire lookout, field biologist, naturalist-educator, graduate school and wilderness ranger in North Cascades National Park. Friends and I started North Cascades Institute in 1986.

These poems celebrate green and misty landscapes and the wilderness they contain. Thanks to the many friends who have accompanied me along the path: Tim McNulty (special thanks to Tim for his keen editorial eye and encouragement), Tom Fleischner, John Horner, Kurt Hoelting, Robert Michael Pyle, Thea Linnaea Pyle, Holly Hughes, Gerry Cook, Hannah Sullivan, Lee Whitford, Libby Mills, Rusty Kuntze, Chris Moench, Jennifer Hahn, John Miles, Rotha Miles, Susan Morgan, Tony Angell, Ken Voorhis, Brian Scheuch, Corinne Hajek, Sterling Clarren, Bruce Underwood, Mary Jean Wiegert, Ed Grumbine, Jeff Hardesty, Tim Jordan, John Dittli, Bob Mierendorf, Bill Lester, Kathleen Dean Moore, Bill Dietrich, Jessica Haag and Julie Toomey.

My family makes all things possible. My parents, Maggie and Irv, and my brother Mark, shared my early path to the mountains. Shelley, Ryan and Teal show me every day why people and place both matter.

NORTH CASCADES INSTITUTE

North Cascades Institute seeks to inspire close relationships with nature through direct experiences in the natural world. Our mission is to conserve and restore Northwest environments through education. Since 1986, the Institute has helped connect people, nature and community through science, art, literature and the hands-on study of the natural and cultural history of the Pacific Northwest. It is critical that we preserve and protect these wild places. The neighborhood wouldn't be the same without them.

To the board of directors and staff of North Cascades Institute – thank you for the passion, skill and commitment you bring to our shared work every day. Your great gift of a sabbatical enabled me to complete this project.

WWW.NCASCADES.ORG

POETRY AVAILABLE FROM PLEASURE BOAT STUDIO:
A LITERARY PRESS

Robert Sund:
Poems from Ish River Country
Taos Mountain
Notes from Disappearing Lake: The River Journals

Red Pine:
P'u Ming's Oxherding Tales and Verses

Tim McNulty:
Ascendance
In Blue Mountain Dusk
Through High Still Air

Tom Jay:
The Blossoms are Ghosts at the Wedding

Mike O'Connor:
The Rainshadow
When the Tiger Weeps
Immortality

Michael Daley:
Moonlight in the Redemptive Forest
The Straits
Original Sin

Denise Banker:
Swimming the Colorado

Finn Wilcox:
Lessons Learned

TO ORDER THESE AND OTHER TITLES FROM PLEASURE
BOAT STUDIO, VISIT: WWW.PLEASUREBOATSTUDIO.COM